M H.

One of a Few

Sgt. Hugh Colhoun.

One of a Few

The Story of a Successful Evasion

by

Hugh Colhoun

The Pentland Press Limited
Edinburgh · Cambridge · Durham

© Hugh Colhoun 1993

First published in 1993 by
The Pentland Press Ltd.
1 Hutton Close
South Church
Bishop Auckland
Durham

ISBN 1 85821 084 4

Typeset by Elite Typesetting Techniques, Southampton.
Printed and bound by Antony Rowe Ltd., Chippenham.

This book is dedicated to the memory of Armand and Marie Esch
and to my other French helpers, whose names I never knew.
Without their help, at great risk to themselves, my escape would
not have been possible.

Contents

Foreword

During World War II the fantastic stories of the very few aircrew who evaded capture after crashing over Germany and Occupied Europe were never told for security reasons and to safeguard those brave families in occupied territory who often risked their lives to help our aircrew. Today those restrictions no longer exist.

Hugh Colhoun's story is one of the most remarkable for two reasons. Firstly his pilot, Flight Lieutenant Harper, crash-landed their crippled Wellington bomber at night, in open countryside, without injuring his crew. A crash landing on a good airfield in daylight calls for high piloting skills, but to do so over unknown territory by the light of the moon was a masterly achievement by the pilot and an unforgettable experience for the crew. Secondly, the crash occurred in Germany rather than in one of the occupied countries and, with no underground organization to help him, Hugh Colhoun escaped from Germany into France after a 12 day trek, and then, with occasional help from some friendly French farmers – at great risk to themselves – he reached Switzerland a further five weeks later.

Hugh Colhoun was 22 years of age at the time. Quietly, unemotionally, and with masterly understatement, he describes the near 500 mile journey from the crash point to Switzerland. The route he followed is shown on the map following. After evacuating the crashed aircraft the crew quickly split up to lessen the chance of being captured. These very young men, in a highly dangerous, hostile environment, were entirely reliant on their own initiative, supported by a dogged determination to avoid capture. They were in Royal Air Force uniform with only a small compass (which was usually hidden in a collar stud) and had an escape pack 'the size of a 50 cigarette tin containing a 2oz. bar of concentrated chocolate, a few Horlicks tablets, a few cigarettes, matches, some water purification tablets and a 12 inch square map of Germany'. Thus equipped Hugh and one other crew member set off together in the dark in the general direction of France.

Resting by day in obscure hiding places, usually with no protection from the weather, travelling on foot by night and avoiding main roads, all towns and villages, and eating root vegetables found in farmers' fields, would have tested the most determined of characters. Great calm, initiative and bravery were shown throughout and he refers, in a very matter of fact way, to how they dealt with one particular occasion when they were stopped and challenged by a German civilian in the Saar area.

After 12 days evading capture in Germany, Hugh and his colleague estimated they had crossed into France and he describes the subsequent help they received from a few French farmers. Unfortunately one farmer they contacted was employing German workers and in the resulting fracas Hugh's colleague was captured, but Hugh made a dramatic escape from the farm. Some seven weeks after the crash he reached neutral Switzerland where he stayed for a lengthy period before he was repatriated to England.

Hugh was the only member of his crew to evade capture and he refers to the harsh treatment which some of his fellow crew members received when they were captured. Aircrew evading capture never asked the names of anyone who helped them for fear of incriminating their helpers if subsequently captured and interrogated. It is therefore delightful to read that after the war Hugh returned to France and found the farm where he first received help. For many years he kept in touch with the farmer and his wife. They are now dead, but Hugh still maintains contact with their children, grandchildren and great grandchildren.

This is a fascinating story that needs to be told and will interest young and old alike. It typifies the spirit which helped to rid Europe of the Nazi dictatorship.

Air Marshal Sir Ivor Broom, KCB., CBE., DSO., DFC., AFC.

List of Illustrations

Frontispiece: Sgt. Hugh Colhoun

The Escape Route
Sketch map showing approximate route taken from Germany to Switzerland.

Early Days

My first flight in an aeroplane took place in about 1932 when Alan Cobham's Air Circus visited Londonderry and I managed to scrape together the necessary 7s. 6d. for a short flight around the airfield. This was a very exciting experience for a 12 year old lad and perhaps it instilled in me the desire to do more flying. However, little did I dream then that 10 years later I would be flying over Germany as an observer in an R.A.F. bomber.

During the Second World War there was no conscription in Northern Ireland and so in 1940 I volunteered to join the R.A.F. with the hope of being selected as a member of an aircrew. After a wait of several months I was sent to Babbacombe and then to Cambridge to do my initial training courses. Once the preliminaries were over I was posted to No. 10 Air Observer School at Dumfries in October 1941 to get down to the task of becoming an observer.

The course covered dead reckoning (DR) and astro-navigation, wireless telegraphy, aerial photography, bombing and gunnery. The aircraft used for this work included the de Havilland Dragon Rapide (a biplane), the Avro Anson, Fairy Battle and Blackburn Botha – quite a collection. Our flying training was carried out over Scotland, the Lake District and the Irish Sea as far as the Isle of Man and the east coast of Northern Ireland. The training programme was quite hectic but very interesting and I enjoyed it immensely. My fellow students on the course, including a large number of Polish officers, were an excellent bunch and there was great comradeship between us.

When invasion rumours were rife in 1941 we were also obliged to do some infantry training in order to assist in the protection of our airfield should the occasion arise. This involved 'bayonet' practice with pikes and dummy soldiers, throwing hand grenades, using our Browning guns on fixed mountings and unarmed combat which, as later events turned out, proved to be extremely useful.

Although we received instruction in the technique of parachute jumping we did not make an actual jump because it was considered too costly to risk injury to aircrew at this time. However, an opportunity to make a real jump occurred in December 1941 during a serious incident which I remember well. It happened while we were on a navigation exercise in a Rapide piloted by Sgt. Junod, an American who had volunteered for service with the R.A.F. before the U.S. entered the war. We were flying towards Northern Ireland and had been told to return to base if we met up with the thick cloud and bad weather that was rolling in towards Scotland. As expected, the cloud caught up with us and I reminded the pilot that he should turn back, which he proceeded to do. Moments later, as I worked out our return course, I realized that the plane had stalled. To my surprise the pilot ordered us to bale out. First of all we had to get our parachutes which were stowed at the rear of the aircraft and which were now overhead as the plane spun towards the ground. It was an impossible task. I released the door catch ready for the jump but despite frantic efforts against the force of gravity we failed to reach our parachutes and so we could only wait and hope. In his panic the pilot had left his seat and was lying half in and half out of the cockpit. However, a miracle happened. The pilot seemed to come to his senses, grabbed the control column and so pulled the aircraft out of its dive. He scrambled back into his seat regaining control just in time, as we were by then only a few hundred feet above the hills of Bonnie Scotland.

When we arrived back at base we were interrogated on the incident. My opinion was that the pilot had not trusted his instruments while in the cloud, had stalled the plane and then failed to carry out the correct drill to bring the plane back under control. After that the pilot was known as 'Spinning J'.

By the 12th May 1942 the course had finished and I had qualified as an observer with an above average rating. I had been in the R.A.F. for more than a year but had not had any leave and, with thoughts of home, expected that my time had arrived. This, however, was not to be and the C.O. informed three of us that we were being posted directly to an operational squadron and that we could ask for leave when we arrived there. (Normally pilots, observers, wireless operators and gunners went to Operational Training Units from their various training schools. Here they were formed into crews and flew together to gain experience before being posted to an operational squadron as a crew.) Two of us were sent to Bourn near Cambridge, to join 101 Squadron which was to suffer some of the heaviest losses of the war. When we asked for leave our expectations were again dashed as our new C.O. was not very sympathetic and said that we would get a week's leave when we had completed five operational trips. When one reflects on the chances of coming through the first five missions it was rather a harsh decision.

After joining 101 Squadron, which was equipped with Mk III Wellington bombers, I made a number of training flights on which I familiarized myself with this type of plane and its equipment. Many of these flights were carried out at night. At this stage in the war the Wellington, along with the Whitley, was the mainstay of the R.A.F. night attacks on Germany.

Soon I became the observer in Sgt. Mahoney's crew which had already undertaken a number of bombing raids over Germany. It was whilst waiting to start my operational flying that the first 1,000 bomber raid was carried out on Cologne. On that night every available aircraft was called into service but, unfortunately, our plane was under repair and so we were unable to participate in this historic raid. Shortly afterwards, on the 6th June, the Day of Judgement arrived and we were briefed to go on what was to be my first operational trip. There was no straightforward leaflet-dropping initiation for me, our target was the German naval base at Emden. As one can imagine I was a little apprehensive as to what sort of 'welcome' I might expect on my first sortie over enemy territory. However, I had little time before take-off to think about what might happen. As the observer I had to obtain the latest meteorological data, instructions on estimated time of arrival (ETA) and height over the target so as to prepare the flight plan. I also had to know the signals of the day in order to identify our aircraft, should it be challenged by one of our own night fighters when approaching the English coast on our return journey. A further duty was to check the bomb load. Once in the air the observer was kept fully occupied too. Unreliable met. data caused problems and on the way to the target much time was spent checking the wind speed and direction by radio fixes, drift observations, etc. In the early war years the observer's duty included not only navigation but also the aiming and dropping of bombs. Hence on the run-in to the target normal navigation had to be suspended while the bombs were dropped and until the aircraft was clear of the target area. Later on the duties of the observer were divided between navigator and bomb aimer. Although no bombing mission can be described as easy, my first encounter with the enemy appeared relatively uneventful. Perhaps it was a case of 'where ignorance is bliss 'tis folly to be wise'!

Two nights later we were off to bomb Essen in the heavily defended industrial Ruhr, known affectionately as 'happy valley' because of the heavy defences in the area. It was quite a daunting experience to see the many searchlight beams scanning the sky which one tried to avoid at all costs. Also there were streams of coloured tracer ammunition and shell bursts all around. It was not only the 'fireworks' display which made me remember this trip: after bombing our target and resuming my navigational duties I noticed on my compass that instead of flying on a westerly course for home we were heading due north, right up the middle of Germany. On querying this with the pilot he said that his instruments showed that he was steering a westerly course. However, on further investigation it transpired that the pilot was steering by his gyroscope and that this had toppled while we had been taking evasive action and consequently was giving a false reading. Fortunately, after making some navigational adjustments we were soon able to get back on the right course for base but just imagine how I felt on only my second trip. I was certainly in at the deep end.

Speaking about the 'deep end' reminds me of an occasion when we carried out a search in the North Sea. Quite often crews could not make it back to base and had to ditch in the sea. It then fell to other crews to carry out a square search of the area where the aircraft was said to have come down. On one of these assignments we spent some four hours searching without finding any survivors. Although not classed as an operational mission it could be dangerous when one considers that it was carried out in daylight and often close to the enemy coast.

I flew fifteen missions with Sgt. Mahoney before he completed his first tour of duty and after that I joined the crew of Flt. Lt. Harper and went on six missions with him. In all, my trips comprised the naval targets of Emden, Bremen and Wilhelmshaven; the industrial towns of Essen, Duisburg, Hamburg, Dusseldorf, Frankfurt, Kassel, Osnabruck, Saarbrucken and Nuremberg and mining trips to the Friesian Islands, Juist and the Baltic.

On two occasions night fighters attacked us. Once when returning from Frankfurt we came under fire from an enemy aircraft near Mons. After a brief skirmish we managed to elude our attacker and return home safely. On the other occasion whilst returning from a raid on Saarbrucken a Junkers 88 attacked us near the Dutch coast. Although quite badly damaged, particularly on the tailplane near the vital elevator hinges, again we managed to return to base. However, we believed that our return fire had damaged the enemy aircraft and it was hoped that he had not been as lucky as we had.

On returning from this Saarbrucken trip in the early hours of the morning we were told that our crew was to be presented to the Duke of Kent who was visiting R.A.F. Bourn, so, after only a couple of hours' sleep, we had to be spruced up and on parade ready to meet His Royal Highness. It was less than a month after this that the Duke was killed in an air crash in Scotland.

Anti-aircraft fire was always a problem and particularly the heavy, concentrated type. On many trips to the Ruhr we experienced this but the one occasion that made most impact on me was on a mission to Bremen, my sixth operational trip. Our aircraft was very much the target for the guns and searchlights and we had to take a lot of evasive action in an attempt to elude the heavy barrage that was ever too close for comfort. When one actually heard the gunfire one knew that it was very near indeed. Quite a while elapsed, during which time we were diving and weaving to escape the searchlights before we managed to get clear of trouble, but not before being hit by some of the flak that the German defences threw at us. Fortunately we were not 'fatally wounded' and again we made it back to base.

Another type of operation carried out by Bomber Command was that of mining enemy shipping routes. This type of operation was usually entrusted to the more experienced crews as great care had to be taken to locate and pin-point the target area. This was important because our own submarines might also have been operating in the area and it was essential to give our naval comrades the precise details of where we had dropped our mines. As I mentioned earlier I was on three mining operations. Our Baltic trip was not successful and outlines the point made previously that mines had to be dropped with precision. After a long journey which involved flying over Denmark, we encountered 10/10ths cloud and despite descending to about 600 ft. we still could not get a pin-point, and even radio fixes were useless, so we had to abandon our mission and return with our load of two 1500 lb. mines. This illustrates the difficulty of obtaining reliable meteorological data at this time. One can imagine how disappointed and frustrated we all felt after such a long and abortive trip.

In the later stages of the war, Pathfinders were used to locate and light up the target area for the following main bomber force. Before the Pathfinders were formed, the task of identifying and lighting up the target fell to the lot of the more experienced crews. At times this proved none too easy and involved more than one run over the target area. With this the danger was increased as the aircraft was exposed to the enemy for a longer period.

A further variant was to carry both flares and bombs and one needs little imagination to realize that this type of load could result in even more time being spent in the target area and entailed at least two clear runs over the target. As in the case of mines, flares were not dropped unless the target had been positively identified as far as was humanly possible.

During the early days of the war DR navigation, using a Mercator chart, was the main and, on most occasions, the only means of getting to and from the target. Wind speed and direction were necessary components of DR navigation, and as accurate meteorological data was not readily available much time was devoted to updating the information to hand so as to improve its accuracy. Wireless fixes were usually possible, but as the enemy had the potential to interfere with them, they had to be verified with other available information. At this time in the campaign our aircraft were equipped with the Decca navigation system Gee but unfortunately this could also be interfered with as soon as one crossed the enemy coastline. So every encouragement was given to the use of astro-navigation whenever possible. This could not be interfered with by the enemy and was always something one could fall back on when all else failed and such a situation was not an outside chance. By close co-operation with the pilot, who had to keep the aircraft on a steady and level course while a bearing was taken, it was possible to get fixes within ten miles of an actual position and this was indeed good under wartime conditions.

Escape from Germany

My final mission took place on 28th August 1942, shortly after the Squadron had moved from Bourn to Stradishall in Suffolk. There were six of us in our crew that night: Flt. Lt. Peter Harper, pilot; Flt. Sgt. Alan Cook, wireless operator; Flt. Sgt. Jock Skinner, gunner; Flt. Sgt. Jimmy Mullineaux, DFM, gunner; Sgt. Jim Dixon, 2nd pilot under training and myself, observer. We set off for Nuremberg in 'A' for Apple on this long journey of more than 1,000 miles. At first the flight was relatively uneventful and we arrived safely at a position near Mannheim, our turning point, where we then set a due easterly course to our target. Shortly after altering course our port engine failed. I cannot say why this happened because, to the best of my knowledge, we had not been attacked by fighters or anti-aircraft fire. Whatever the reason we had only one engine and our first instinct was to jettison our bombs and turn for home on a north-westerly course. However, the plane would not maintain height so we attempted to lighten our load still further by jettisoning our guns and chopping out our wireless equipment and anything else that we could lay our hands on. To our dismay the plane still continued to drift lower and lower and we were ordered

R.A.F. Station,
STRADISHALL,   Suffolk.

101S/C/509/58/P.1.   30th August, 1942.

Dear Mr. Colhoun,

It was with profound regret that I had to send
you a telegram to inform you that your Son is reported
missing from Air Operations, as the aircraft in which
he was a member of the Crew took off from here on an
Operational Sortie over enemy territory failed to return
to base.

I am unable as yet to give you any news as no
signals were received from the aircraft after take off,
but you will be advised immediately of any information
that comes through, and we all hope that good news will
eventually be received.

Your Son will be greatly missed here as he was
not only a very popular member of the Squadron, but had
proved himself to be a most efficient and competent
Navigator of aircraft.

He had many Operational Sorties to his credit
all of which were carried out with a splendid courage and
devotion to duty.

I should like to express my sincere sympathy
at this time combined with that of the entire Squadron.

Yours sincerely,

Wing Commander, Commanding,
No. 101 Squadron, R.A.F.

Mr. D. Colhoun,
21, Violet Street,
LONDONDERRY,
Northern Ireland.

to put on our parachutes. We were fortunate that our pilot was able to control the aircraft and, it being a bright moonlit night, that he could see the countryside fairly well.

The pilot decided to attempt a crash landing, that is a landing without the wheels of the aircraft being lowered, so we had to take up crash positions lying prone on the floor of the aircraft and bracing ourselves against the main spar to protect us from the impact of landing. Shortly afterwards our plane touched down and we bumped along the ground before coming to a standstill. Thanks to our pilot, who had made a very good belly landing, none of the crew was injured apart from superficial cuts and bruises. The pilot gave orders to abandon the aircraft and we quickly went into action. One of my duties was to ensure that any secret equipment that we carried was destroyed and finally I activated an incendiary device that would set the aircraft alight. The normal exit from a Wellington was via a hatch in the floor of the plane. However, as the aircraft was lying on its belly some of the crew escaped through the canopy over the cockpit while others, including myself, escaped through the astro-dome half way along the top of the fuselage. As the latter was only a relatively small opening it was a tight squeeze but it is wonderful what one can do in an emergency! We all got out safely and found ourselves in the middle of a field of ripe corn which must have been clearly visible to the pilot in the moonlight and which undoubtedly influenced his decision to attempt a landing.

Having left the aircraft our next objective was to get well away from it as quickly as possible because the hunt for us would have already begun. We hurriedly decided to split into three pairs and to try to make our escape. My travelling companion was to be Jim Dixon, who was an Australian. As speed was essential we lost no time in wishing our fellow crew members good luck and getting away from the aircraft as swiftly as we could. It was immaterial at this stage in which direction we went. As we set off, a quick glance at our plane showed that it was already beginning to burn.

Together we made our way across the fields, skirting some woods on the way and at a reasonable distance from the plane we paused to take stock of the situation. From our last known position near Mannheim our rough estimate indicated that we were now probably somewhere north-west of the town. It was therefore decided that we would have to travel in a south-westerly direction to reach France and we used our escape compass, which was concealed in a tunic button, to check on our direction. We continued on our way and crossed some minor roads and as road signs were still in use in Germany, as distinct from the wartime practice of removing them in Britain, we tried to read these in order to ascertain our whereabouts. At our first attempt we heard someone approaching and we threw ourselves down in some long grass beside the road and waited anxiously as the footsteps came nearer. In the semi-darkness the passer-by looked like a German soldier, perhaps returning to his barracks. We were very relieved when he continued on his way obviously unaware of our presence. This incident made us realize at a very early stage just how vigilant one would have to be. We continued walking across country for as long as we could during that first night hoping to make as much ground as possible between ourselves and our burning aircraft. As dawn broke we sought our first refuge in rough scrub just at the edge of a wood.

As we settled down in our hiding place we considered our position. Here we were in Germany, wearing R.A.F. uniform, with no money, speaking not a word of German and with only a compass and one escape pack between us. This escape pack consisted of a box about the size of a 50 cigarette tin which contained a 2 oz. bar of concentrated chocolate, a few Horlicks tablets, a few cigarettes, matches, some water purification tablets and a map of Germany. In the early days of the war these escape maps were approximately 12 inches square and were printed on blue paper with the towns marked in black, and to give you some idea of the scale, Berlin appeared as a small dot. We pondered over this inadequate map in an attempt to ascertain our position, trying to locate some of the names we had seen on the road signs. It was certainly a hit or miss effort but we did manage to find some of the towns although generally they were many miles away.

We decided that as we were in uniform and had no access to any other clothing our strategy must be to walk during the night and find a place in which to hide during the day. Fortunately I was wearing shoes but my partner was wearing loose-fitting flying boots which, as events turned out, made walking difficult and painful for him. We confirmed our intention of travelling in a south-westerly direction and decided that if any difficulties were encountered in following this route we would err on the side of safety and temporarily follow a westerly course, thus hopefully ensuring that we would eventually arrive in France. During these daylight hours we obviously had to keep watch in case anyone spotted us. As for sleeping, we agreed that while one tried to have a nap the other would keep watch. However, in those early days we were not particularly tired and sleep did not bother us. We also tried to survey the surrounding countryside and to spot any difficulties such as forests and rivers, so that we could set off on our next night's walk in a predetermined direction.

Also during the day we indulged in a sumptuous meal of half a Horlicks tablet and half a square of chocolate each.

As darkness approached we set off on our travels again with the simple objective of getting as far away as possible from the scene of the previous night's crash so that the area for the Germans to search would be considerably increased. Again we travelled more or less by our compass and tried to avoid roads, towns and villages. The going was difficult and slow as all the time we were keeping away from habitation to minimize the risk of being spotted. Our one bonus that night was finding some extra food in the form of turnips. Towards dawn we started looking for a possible hiding place for the coming day. This proved somewhat difficult but eventually we found refuge in more rough scrub similar to our first stop and we spent the ensuing day much as we had spent the previous one.

With plenty of time on our hands our thoughts ranged near and far. We wondered how our fellow crew members were getting along and whether they had been captured. We also pondered on how far away, or how near, we were to being caught ourselves. Were the Germans on our trail? Our families at home were much in our minds and we wondered how they were standing up to the bad news. After all, they did not know that we were still alive and free.

Again, as dusk approached, we set off on our night's walk. We noticed in the far distance a lot of flashes which we thought were the result of a bombing raid on some German town but as time went by it turned out to be a severe thunderstorm with almost continuous intense lightning flashes and lots of heavy rain. Later we learned that this part of Germany is noted for these severe storms. As we had no shelter or protective clothing we were soon soaked to the skin but we kept walking until daybreak. Our hide-out for the following day was a very small clearing near the edge of a forest but, as we were completely soaked and the ground was very wet, we spent the day trying to keep ourselves warm by walking around in this clearing and hoping that by night-time we would have dried out. During this day our thoughts were rather mixed. On the one hand we were pleased to be still free but then doubts set in and we wondered whether or not we would get pneumonia. We debated whether our freedom was worthwhile but then reminded ourselves that it was the duty of all aircrew to evade capture and endeavour to return home. By nightfall we had nearly dried out and as we had still not been caught our courage returned and we set off on another night's trek.

Soon we settled down to our routine of walking by night and hiding by day and we considered finding a safe hiding place to be more important than the distance travelled each night. It was difficult to predict what sort of terrain we might come up against as we tried to follow our south-westerly course across the German countryside. Sometimes the going proved very difficult and for short periods we were forced on to minor roads and sometimes railways. One night we came across a railway line and as we scrambled down the cutting in the darkness, we tripped over the signal wires beside the track and, as these wires twanged in the stillness of the night, we feared that someone might hear the noise but fortunately all remained peaceful. Walking along railway lines, while quite easy, required a slight alteration to one's step as the sleepers never seemed to be the right distance apart! However, this was a problem that we easily overcame. Of course, one had to be on the alert for trains and at various times they made their inevitable appearance. When this happened we had to lie down beside the track, two or three feet from the rails, while a train hurtled by making a thunderous and terrifying noise. It may be difficult to imagine what this was like unless one has experienced it.

Jim told me that he had jumped trains in Australia and he suggested that it might be possible for us to try this. If successful, we would be able to make much more headway with less effort. The plan was to hide near the track on the departure side of a station and when a goods train was under way we would run after it and, hopefully, pull ourselves up on to a wagon before it got up speed. This was the theory but in practice the trains always seemed to pick up speed too quickly and although we ran after a number of trains my friend, who was the expert and whom I always allowed to go first, never caught one!

Travelling along a railway line did provide the odd bonus. For example I can recall my companion once finding a glowing ember in the middle of the track from which he was able to light his cigarette. Whilst this made his day, or night, I was not interested, being a non-smoker. Jim Dixon's craving for a cigarette was very worrying especially as on one occasion, when near an isolated railway station, he contemplated asking a passenger for a light. I had to remind him of the danger he would be putting us both in by approaching anyone, particularly as he was still in uniform and spoke no German.

One night, after walking along a forest path, the time had come for us to seek our usual dawn hide-out where we could rest, eat our meagre rations and try to work out our position but the only place we could find was amongst the trees. Unfortunately it was a mature forest with no undergrowth and it was possible to see for a considerable distance between the lines of trees – not an ideal hiding place. As daylight broke we were horrified to see forestry workers arriving and they began work some 50 to 100 yards away from us. They worked throughout the day and we had to ensure that we kept very still and well hidden behind the rows of trees. It was a very uncomfortable and nerve-racking experience and the day seemed never ending. When evening approached and the workers left we heaved a great sigh of relief.

Once again as darkness fell we were off on our travels but as we had now been walking for quite a number of nights we found that the going was becoming more difficult and it took some time to get our feet warmed up and working. We were very foot-weary and had to rest frequently and I can well remember our sitting down beside a haycock in the middle of a field and both of us nodding off to sleep for a while. This was indeed dangerous because of the possibility of being caught off guard.

In this part of Germany the terrain was very difficult and again we were fortunate in being able to travel along a railway line. On one eventful night we were coming along the track and without much warning we suddenly found ourselves at the entrance to a marshalling yard. Almost as quickly, we were challenged by someone standing up in a wagon some yards away. We could see this figure silhouetted against the sky and instinctively threw ourselves flat between the tracks just in case he might shoot at us. Things happened very quickly and as luck would have it a train came between him and us and this presented us with the opportunity to run along the track for some hundred yards and get off the railway. However, we now found ourselves on a road leading towards a town. This was something which we had always tried to avoid but circumstances dictated otherwise. After a short distance the road passed under the railway line and this enabled us to cross the railway and resume walking in a general south-westerly direction and gave us the opportunity of keeping away from the town. It was probably Dillingen or another of the Saar towns.

After a short distance we met a man coming in the opposite direction who challenged us with what we believed to be a pistol. I am not sure how he recognized us so readily as it was still fairly dark. Maybe we did not give the Hitler salute or perhaps he noticed our uniforms or Jim's flying boots which made him suspicious. As he pointed the gun and beckoned us to walk we had little choice but to do just that. However, I realized that if we were to escape we must do something quickly and I recalled some of the advice on unarmed combat which I had received during training. So we kept talking to our captor in English while he gabbled away in German, the idea being to disturb his concentration. At the same time I purposely kept my back very close to him so that I was able to bring my raised arms down suddenly, knocking his arm aside and at the same time grabbing the gun. This was the unarmed combat technique which I had been taught and which was designed to ensure that at worst one might only receive a superficial injury, perhaps on the arm or shoulder. On grabbing the 'gun' we discovered it to be a tobacco pipe for which we were extremely thankful. I immediately hit out at our captor and off we sprinted down the road as fast as our feet would carry us. On reflection I believe he may have been a railway worker on his way to start an early morning shift.

Although we were still free we had, in the space of a short time, twice alerted the Germans to our presence and our aim was to get well away from this main road and to make as much ground as possible. However, this proved difficult and after a few hundred yards we were still unable to get off the

road and found ourselves at a river bridge, probably over the
Saar. Having little choice we made haste to cross it and
although we saw one or two people, possibly on their way to
work, fortunately they did not take any notice of us in the
semi-darkness. As soon as we had crossed the bridge we were
able to leave the road and get into the countryside once more.
Needless to say we picked up speed to get as far away as
possible from the scene of the night's incidents. As dawn
broke we looked for some suitable refuge in which to hide
and in view of the happenings of the previous night it was
essential to find some good undergrowth in which to lie low.
The following day was again spent trying to rest but we had
to keep very much on the alert and did not get any sleep. We
ate some more turnip, a few crab-apples which we had found
growing along the roadside and a Horlicks tablet to keep the
pangs of hunger away.

Our water supply during the past week or so had been taken
from streams and, on a few occasions, from the fountains in
some of the very small villages through which we had passed
on our nightly walks. Sometimes in these villages we nearly
jumped out of our skins when the church clock unexpectedly
chimed the hour, breaking the eerie silence.

The next night we had some very difficult ground to cover
and again we were thankful that we had a railway line to help
us on our way. At one point the track seemed to traverse
gorges and we were not quite sure whether the area was
guarded or not. On reflection this may have been part of the
Siegfried Line fortifications. Later we passed through a very
small village consisting of a few farmhouses. Just as we
reached the last one we were aware of a dog barking and
naturally we hurried along just in case we had aroused suspicions. It was very unusual to hear a dog bark in Germany and

we could not recall hearing one previously. Possibly there were not many dogs because of the shortage of food for them.

During our next day's rest we considered our position and thought that if we had not already crossed the French border then we must be very near to it. However, we were not sure of the difficulties involved in crossing the Siegfried and Maginot Lines and we debated whether we could have negotiated them without realizing it. To be on the safe side we decided to walk for a couple more nights to make absolutely sure that we were in France before seeking assistance.

After travelling for two more nights we decided that the time had come to seek help. It was now twelve days since we had landed in Germany and we were tired, hungry and our feet very sore, especially those of my companion who had been walking in his flying boots. Our hiding place that day was a small coppice and from there we had a good view of the surrounding countryside. We spotted an isolated farmhouse where we thought we might find food and shelter. It seemed well situated, for, should anything untoward happen, we would have a fifty-fifty chance of getting away without being caught. As darkness began to fall we moved closer to the farm. About 9 o'clock when we reckoned that any farm workers would have gone home, and only the family would be around, we decided to take the plunge.

Alone in France

We moved quietly towards the farmhouse and tapped gently on the door. As we waited in trepidation, wondering what might happen next, a downstairs window opened and the farmer demanded to know who was there. We replied in our best schoolboy French telling him that we were R.A.F. escapers who had been walking for two weeks and that we were seeking help. He unbolted the door and beckoned us in. We then had to convince the farmer and his wife that we were genuine. One has to remember that the Germans, and particularly the Gestapo, posed as escapers in order to trap would-be helpers and the penalty for giving such help would have been deportation to a concentration camp or death. If our hosts were difficult to convince this was quite understandable. One of our problems was that having crashed in Germany we had no proof of our story. Had we landed in France the Resistance Movement would have known and they would have been on the look out for the crew. Of course, we were still wearing our uniforms and had our identity discs and doubtless, being unshaven and unkempt, we looked the part having been on the run for so long. Our story must have been convincing as we were allowed to stay.

One of their first priorities was to give us some food and what a treat it was to have something to eat once again. Later we were shown to an upstairs bedroom and here we enjoyed a good night's sleep, the first we had had for nearly a fortnight. We were told that we had to remain in the bedroom during daylight hours as it was absolutely essential that we should not be seen by the farm workers. The next morning we were introduced to the farmer's three teenage daughters with whom we tried to converse with the aid of a dictionary. We discovered that we were at Rinange, near Boulay, and less than 10 miles from the German border. So we had been prudent to continue our journey for another two nights after we thought we had crossed the frontier.

During our stay we were able to have a wash and shave and generally clean ourselves up. It was also a great relief to rest our weary feet and soon we began to feel human again. We were indeed lucky to have found such a haven. After two nights' rest at Rinange it was time to set off on our travels again. But this time we were slightly better equipped. Our hosts had given us a Michelin map, some food and a cornsack each which we could use as a sleeping bag. I had also acquired a French beret and an old jacket to cover my battledress and provide extra warmth.

Although we had reached our first objective, France, we were still intent on travelling in a south-westerly direction hoping, eventually to reach Spain. Of course Spain was several hundred miles away but we considered that there was now the possibility of obtaining some help from the Resistance Movement along the way. Switzerland was much nearer but Jim did not think that we would be able to cross the Rhine and this was no time to argue.

We bade farewell to the friends who had given us so much

help not even knowing their names. I made it a rule never
to ask for names nor make a note of addresses so that whatever happened I could not betray those who had helped me.
As we left the farm our host accompanied us and took us
towards Charleville where he put us on the right road. With
the aid of our map we were now able to plan our route
more easily, avoiding such obstacles as towns and rivers
although we knew that at some point in the near future we
would have to cross the Moselle, which was quite a large
river.

We resolved to continue walking for several nights until
our food supply was exhausted before seeking further help.
Our general route towards the Moselle was via Les Etangs,
Jury and Fleury. South of Metz we reached the banks of the
river. As the Moselle was wide we were obviously unable to
swim across and so we had to find some other means of
getting over. From the map we could see that the first bridge
on our route was at Pont-à-Mousson. However, we did not
wish to cross there as it was a fairly large town so we continued southward hoping to find another bridge at some small
village. After a while we came to a bridge, possibly at
Dieulouard, which we reconnoitred to make sure that it was
not guarded. Luck was not with us, a dog began barking and
this suggested to us that it was aware of our presence, so we
hastily abandoned that crossing and continued along the bank
hoping that another opportunity would present itself fairly
soon. It was slow going, walking along the river bank in the
dark, but eventually we came to another bridge which may
have been at Marbache. We watched carefully for some time
to see if there was any sign of life and being satisfied that all
was well we began to cross slowly and quietly. About half
way over we came to a small hut, or sentry box, showing a

chink of light from its slightly open door. It was obviously occupied so we took to our heels and reached the other side without delay, not stopping on the far bank to see if anybody had spotted us. We had safely crossed the Moselle.

It was about this time that Jim suggested that it would be a good idea if we could find a farmer who would be willing to let us sleep in his barn during the day and perhaps supply us with some food, thus getting away from the necessity of sleeping rough. I was not very enamoured of this scheme but for the sake of harmony I agreed to go along with the idea to see how things would turn out. My main objection was that we would arrive at a farm about dawn and this would coincide with the arrival of farm workers and, in my opinion, would not be the best time to ask the farmer for help. However, we decided to have a go and picked what we thought was a suitable place near Flirey. Just before dawn we knocked at the farmhouse door and told the farmer in our halting French who we were and asked for help. He called one of his workers over and put us in his charge and we assumed that we would be taken to a barn where we could hide for the day. The farm worker took us to a cowshed and beckoned us to enter. My friend entered first and I then followed but noticed that the farm worker was trying to close the door on us. At that moment I realized that this was an unfriendly farm and that we were in trouble. I immediately stuck my foot in the door to prevent it being closed and then wrenched it open, pushing our would-be captor aside as I made haste to escape. During this time I did not know what Jim was doing. I had hoped that he would have been trying to help me, or at least have been making his escape while I was tackling the farm worker. But this seems not to be the case. I ran across the farmyard, tripped over some implement, picked myself up in a flash and broke the world sprint record as I ran up the road away from the farm. I was aware of one or two people standing around as I made my dash for freedom. At what I judged to be a safe distance I hid in a hedge and waited to see if my friend had escaped and had followed me. As there was no sign of him after quite a long wait, I deemed it prudent to get on my way and to find a safe haven for the ensuing day. As always on these occasions it was essential to make as much ground as possible before daylight arrived. I eventually settled down in some undergrowth beside a river and prepared to spend the day resting and planning my future journey. Fortunately I still had the Michelin map and after studying it carefully realized that it was possible to reach Switzerland without crossing the Rhine. I decided that this would be my objective rather than continuing the long trek to Spain. Whilst sad at having lost my companion it did simplify my decision making now that I had only myself to please. I reflected on the recent incident and wondered what had happened to Jim.

I had not been in my refuge for more than an hour or so when, to my consternation, a keen fisherman appeared on the river bank and settled down to do a day's fishing only a few feet from where I was hidden. I was forced to keep very still and very much on the alert in case I drew attention to my presence. After what seemed an eternity he packed up and departed much to my relief both mentally and physically. These last two incidents were unpredictable and demonstrate that one had to act quickly in such circumstances. They also illustrate that there is more than an element of luck in all successful escapes.

Soon it was time for me to start walking on my own for the first time. I continued in the same routine and after walking for a few more nights I decided to look for assistance again, particularly as I was in need of food.

I spied out a farm and as darkness fell I knocked on the door and asked for help. This was the home of a young farmer, his wife and children. I told my story of having crashed in Germany and of walking to France and they listened carefully and quizzed me keenly. Eventually they agreed that I could stay for the night. However, after some time it was obvious that their suspicions had not completely gone and they started questioning me again. I could quite understand their doubts and the difficulties that this young farmer was experiencing in allowing me to stay, knowing what ruses the occupying German forces engaged in. Finally they let me stay and found me a bed. I remained with this family during the following day and as darkness fell the next night I thanked the farmer for his help and faith in me and was on my way again, feeling rested and carrying food for a few more days. I continued my lone walk heading southward between Commercy and Toul, choosing this route so as to avoid the large town of Nancy. Around the Gondrecourt area my direction was more south-easterly and my walk took me somewhere between Mirecourt and Vittel as I travelled towards Dompaire.

Having walked for four or five nights since receiving my last help I decided to seek food and shelter again. As was my practice, at nightfall I selected a farmhouse on the outskirts of a very small village. I was received by the genial farmer and his family and after hearing my story they seemed to believe me without question and allowed me to stay the night. I enjoyed a good meal before having a restful sleep. In the morning the farmer indicated that he would help me on my way by taking me in his horse-drawn cart in the general direction that I was travelling. My first thought was that I would be on the road in daylight which was against my principles and filled me with apprehension. However, with some food which the farmer had kindly given me safely tucked away in my sack, I climbed up on the cart beside the driver and off we went. I added another phrase to my French vocabulary as every now and then the farmer would urge his horse on by saying *'Allez oup!'* As we jogged along the road I was dismayed to see a column of German army vehicles coming towards us. I certainly felt very uneasy but I must have looked like a typical Frenchman in my black beret and old jacket as we passed them without incident. After about half an hour the farmer put me down at the side of the road and wished me *'bonne chance'*. I thanked him very much for all his help and hastily made my way off the road and across the fields. It was a little disconcerting to be out in daylight in flat open country with little cover. There were people working in the fields so I just moved as quickly as possible without drawing attention to myself in the hope of finding some suitable hiding place for the rest of the day. Fortunately I had no problems and was soon settled in a good hide-out.

During the next night's trek I came to a canal which I had to cross, I think this was at Dompaire, and I can remember resting on the canal bank in the middle of the night. Fortunately there was a small bridge and so the canal presented no difficulty.

I continued to trudge along making my way slowly towards Switzerland. The going was fairly easy at this stage. Sometimes I travelled across open country and at other times along minor roads. Occasionally I even dared to wander through small villages, their main streets lined with typical French farmhouses accommodating both family and animals and each with its large heap of manure outside. These villages usually had a fountain of running water from which I was able to quench my thirst.

Sometimes I found myself in very odd circumstances and on one occasion can remember sitting on a cemetery wall in the moonlight eating some meagre rations. In my younger days had I passed a cemetery at night I would have taken to my heels and run like the devil! However, things were very different in 1942.

On my travels I was constantly searching for food such as vegetables and fruit, ripe or unripe. One moonlit night I came across a vineyard and I ventured in, crawling along between the low rows of vines, searching for any ripe grapes. I did find a few reasonably edible ones but I also found someone else with similar ideas. I spotted the silhouette of someone doing much the same as myself and consequently I had to lie low and keep a close watch on events. I was puzzled as to his identity, he may have been a tramp in search of food, or who knows, he may have been a fellow escaper, but needless to say I did not trouble to find out. Instead I waited until he had gone before I emerged from the vineyard and continued on my way.

My next port of call in search of rest and food was a very small, primitive cottage at an isolated railway level-crossing. The middle-aged husband and wife who lived there listened to my story and obviously believing it they allowed me to stay for twenty-four hours. Apart from being given food it was always nice to have a wash and to rest one's tired feet. It transpired that the wife was the level-crossing keeper and she opened and closed the gates when she received a signal from a bell that rang in the cottage. Again my hosts were very pleasant but they were adamant that I remained inside the cottage during daylight hours although I never saw anyone around while I was there.

As dusk fell the next evening I left the little cottage with a few provisions to help me on my lonesome way. Being alone never seemed to bother me, I suppose my mind was so preoccupied with self-preservation that I did not have time to think about being lonely.

During my long trek I seem to have been lucky with the weather and, apart from the thunderstorm in Germany, cannot recall any period when it was really bad. The temperature was quite reasonable during the day, probably about the average for the time of year, but as the end of September arrived it was noticeable that the nights were getting colder. However, I still had my cornsack which helped to keep out the cold and so proved very useful.

I was fortunate that I had remained reasonably fit since landing in Germany. Apart from the inevitable loss of weight my only real problems were my very sore feet and an abscess on my chest.

I continued on my way on a route that took me between Darney and Epinal in the general direction of Xertigny. Nothing very significant happened and after another few nights of walking and days of hiding I was ready to seek help again. This time I picked a little wooden house, not much more than a shack, on a market garden. Here I found an old lady and her son who worked the land for his living. As always I told my story as best I could in my limited French and again I seemed to have convinced them that I was genuine. They took me in and I enjoyed some food, a rest and again the opportunity to have a refreshing wash. I stayed the night and during the next day the old lady gave me a cup of tea, saying that she was sure that I would like some English tea. It was indeed a very kind thought but I was somewhat disappointed when the drink turned out to be mint tea. It impressed me that my helpers were always prepared to share their food with me for it has to be remembered that food was short in France and that sometimes they did not even get their due rations.

Again at nightfall I bade farewell to my hosts and set off on the next stage of my journey. After a few more nights of relatively uneventful walking I came to my next stop which was once again a smallholding. At this house I found an old lady, her married son and his wife and a young child of about a year. I told them my story and they took me in and once again I enjoyed a meal and a bed.

The next day we were discussing my escape and the son suggested that if I stayed another night he would introduce me to an English speaking school teacher who might be able to offer me some help. That evening I duly met this lady. She had lived in England and spoke good English which helped considerably. She questioned me at length and said that if I remained yet another night she would arrange for me to meet Monsieur Blanc. At this point I thought that perhaps I was going to get some help from the Resistance Movement. This was the first occasion that there had been any suggestion of such help, although this was understandable as having crashed in Germany there was no proof of my story. That night I went to bed with great expectations of meeting Monsieur Blanc the following day. But it was not to be. In the early hours, perhaps about one or two o'clock in the morning we were awakened by a loud bang. The R.A.F. were presumably bombing somewhere nearby and a stray bomb had dropped sufficiently close to the house to damage it. In fact the ceilings had been brought down and the place was

covered in plaster. My helper said that it would be best for me
to leave as the gendarmes would be there in the morning to
inspect the damage and, of course, it would be unwise for me
to be found there. He gave me a little food and off I went into
the night. How fate strikes – this was my one chance of some
help from the Resistance and it was frustrated, probably by an
R.A.F. bomb. Having left my last helper rather hurriedly and
unexpectedly I just continued walking until dawn. I found
myself a hide-out for the day where I spent the time review-
ing my situation and doing some planning for the route ahead.
Since passing Xertigny my route had been between Bains and
Plombieres, near Fougerolles, avoiding Luxeuil and then in
the direction of Ronchamp. By now I was nearing Switzerland and from my map I could see that the town of Delle was
very near to the frontier and that my general route should be
in that direction.

It had been a long time since crashing in Germany and I
had walked very many weary miles with many incidents *en
route*. However, I was lucky that I had remained free all this
time. Having come such a long way, and now that I was
nearing my goal of entering Switzerland, I was more than
ever determined not to be captured. It would have been un-
thinkable to have been caught near the Swiss frontier and for
all the efforts of the past six weeks to have been in vain.

My route took me near Hericourt and then in a more easterly direction towards Bourogne and then I followed the road
towards Grandvillars. Between Grandvillars and Joncherey I
found myself a good refuge for the day and there I contemplated my crossing of the Swiss frontier during the following
night. I had little idea of what a frontier looked like and
whether it would be guarded or not. My mind wandered back
to my days in the Boy Scouts and I recalled my Scoutmaster

telling a story of the First World War where troops had to scale masses of barbed wire. To me this seemed a possibility although I had no idea how I would scale barbed wire. Anyhow, I considered that my fate was very much in the lap of the gods and all that I could do was to take reasonable precautions and not do anything silly. I made up my mind that as soon as darkness began to fall I would make an early attempt on the frontier.

I continued along the road and passed through the small village of Joncherey which I knew to be only a few miles from the border. As I walked along I could see the lights of Switzerland in the distance. I had to be particularly careful that I did not go anywhere near the town of Delle and kept well away from it by diverging in a more easterly direction away from the road. Having ensured that I had kept away from Delle I continued towards Switzerland. My route was over some fields and then I encountered a wood. This was rather disconcerting as I did not know its extent and one cannot easily walk through a wood without making some noise as dry, brittle twigs snap underfoot. However, my luck was in and after a very short distance I was out in the open once more. The first sign of the frontier was a large notice 'Zone Interdit'. So from this point I had to be extremely careful as I did not know what lay between me and safety. I crossed a field and as I walked along I came to a small opening on to a country lane and the only barrier to this track was a single strand of barbed wire. I stepped over this very carefully and continued down the narrow laneway.

I now found myself at the edge of the village of Boncourt which I was reasonably sure was Swiss because of its lights. I paused at the end of this track pondering what my next move should be. The choice seemed to be to give myself up at this point or to try to make my way to Berne and the British Legation. While I was cogitating I saw a Swiss policeman not very far off and this made up my mind for me. I went up to him and in my best French told him who and what I was. He may have been a little surprised but seemed very friendly and he took me along to the local police chief's home in the village. On arrival I told the chief very briefly who I was but his first thoughts seemed to be to get me some food rather than to interrogate me. I can recall the wonderful meal of ham and eggs which I relished.

When it came to the interrogation I told him that our plane had crash-landed in Germany and that about ten days later we had been captured for a short while by a German civilian. I also told him of the incident in France when I became separated from my companion. I recounted how I had been on my own for the rest of the journey and after a period of about six or seven weeks I had made my way to Switzerland.

It was by now late and time for bed. My bedroom turned out to be a small cell in the police chief's house and the bed a sloping platform on which was a bean-bag. However, this did not worry me as it was luxury compared with what I had experienced in recent weeks. I was locked up for the night but I was safe at last.

Swiss Interlude

In the morning, having had some breakfast, I was taken across the road to the local military barracks where I enjoyed a good shower. The army personnel were extremely kind and they shaved me and gave me a haircut and kitted me out with clean underclothing, socks and a shirt. Soon I began to feel quite civilized again. Later I learned that a Swiss soldier had even taken the trouble to send, unofficially, a postcard to my parents informing them that I had arrived safely in Switzerland.

I was taken for a walk in the village and the soldiers asked me where I had crossed the border. When I told them they explained to me that there was no permanent guard on the frontier at that point but that it was patrolled by German soldiers with dogs on the French side. They thought I had been very lucky to get safely across.

Later that day I was taken further into Switzerland to Porrentruy where I was put in the local civilian prison. Each prisoner was allocated a cell where he was locked up at night but during the day the time was spent in a fairly large common room with other prisoners. My fellow inmates seemed to be there for petty crimes, some of which involved the

Luftpost
Par avion - Via aerea

HUTTWIL (Bern) – STÄDTLIPLATZ

POSTKARTE CARTE POSTALE CARTOLINA POSTALE

HELVETIA 50

Sender
JOHN FINSTERWALD
HASELSTRASSE
BADEN
SWITZERLAND

Mr & Mrs
COLHOUN
21 VIOLET STREET
LONDONDERRY
NORTH – IRELAND

BADEN 16-10-42
16 HASELSTRASSE

Mr. and Mrs. Colhoun
LONDONDERRY

Please receive the good news that your
son Hugh is safe in Switzerland.
He escaped from Germany and will
stay here for the time being. He will
communicate with you at the earliest
possible moment.
        Sincerely yours
                John Finsterwald
                a swiss soldier.

smuggling of food from Switzerland into France. I had no reading material so most of my time was spent attempting to converse with my fellow prisoners. The food in prison was very meagre. We were given black coffee for breakfast with a ration of bread which had to last all day. For lunch we were given a bowl of soup, usually meat soup, and again a drink of black coffee in the evening. It was certainly a sparse diet but in the circumstances it was perhaps best for me having gone so long with just the minimum of food.

Time went on and I had heard nothing from the British authorities in Switzerland nor, indeed, from the Swiss authorities as to how long I was going to remain in prison. I began to get a little impatient. I did not really know if the British Legation were aware of my presence in Switzerland so I decided that by some means or other I must try to let them know. I managed to write a brief note which I addressed to the British Legation in Berne and I asked one of the prisoners who was being discharged to post it for me. Within a few days things began to happen but I do not know if this was due to my letter or merely coincidental. After ten days of imprisonment at Porrentruy I was taken to another prison at Délémont. Here I encountered many Jewish refugees but I did not learn much about their background as I was only there for one night.

Early next morning a Swiss army officer collected me and took me by train to the Army Headquarters in Berne. I can recall sitting in the train looking a little like a tramp, still wearing my dirty battledress and shoes that were nearly worn away, complete with my rolled up cornsack. I had made several attempts to rid myself of this sack since entering Switzerland but in the end it accompanied me all the way to the British Legation. I also vividly recall walking across the

bridge in Berne early that morning with my officer escort and
I am sure there were many eyes cast in my direction. We soon
reached the Military Headquarters where I was finally interrogated by the Swiss Army. My story was as before high-
lighting my capture because, according to the Geneva Con-
vention, an escaper is entitled to his freedom in a neutral
country. When the questioning was finished I was told that I
would be collected by a member of the British Legation. In
due course Major Fryer, the Assistant Military Attaché, arrived and took me by car to the Legation. Here I was interrogated by the Air Attaché, Air Commodore Freddie West, VC,
and by the Military Attaché, Colonel Cartwright. They questioned me in great detail about my escape from the moment of
the crash in Germany to the day of my arrival in Switzerland.
During the interview Colonel Cartwright was particularly interested to know how I had crossed the Siegfried and Maginot
Lines, as this information could have been of use to other
escapers. Unfortunately, I was unable to give him much help
as all my walking had been done at night and, therefore, I had
never been able to get a comprehensive view of the area
through which I was walking.

Later that day I was taken to buy some new clothes at a
store in Berne and so once again I looked respectable. Next,
accommodation was arranged for me at the family-run Pen-
sion Herter in the Kramgasse.

On the night of my arrival in Berne there was a small
private party being given at the home of Freddie West to
which I was invited. Also at the party were a number of
Colditz escapers including Pat Reid, Bill Stephens, Hank
Wardle and Ronnie Littledale, who had themselves just arrived in Switzerland. Soon we were swapping stories of our
respective escapes and I was surprised that they thought that

my escape had been more difficult than theirs. The reason they gave was that they had spent many months planning their escape and had learnt German. They had been provided with false papers, had civilian clothing and money and so had set off well prepared. Whereas in my case I had landed in the middle of enemy territory with none of those things and simply had to use my initiative.

Later the same evening we all went on to another party at the United States Air Attaché's home, so my first night of freedom was a night to remember and quite a shock to my system which had gone without much food over the past couple of months.

On that first night I also met the Minister and his wife, Mr. and Mrs. Clifford Norton, Major Fryer's wife and a number of the Legation staff. Mrs. Fryer said that if I wished to call at their flat in Berne at any time I would be most welcome. She said that the maid would make me tea and that there was plenty of reading material which would help pass the time. So during my first few weeks in Berne I availed myself of this very kind offer.

I was also able to explore the city. The main shopping streets were lined with ancient buildings fronted by arcades and the shop windows displayed a large array of goods, unlike the shops I had left behind in wartime Britain. The many colourful sixteenth century fountains and the *zeitglockenturm*, or clock tower, also added to the medieval appearance of the town. This clock always attracted an audience, especially at midday, to witness the line of mechanical bears marching around a sitting figure as the hour was struck. The heraldic emblem of Berne is a bear and one could find real live ones in the famous bearpit near the Nydeggbrucke. The Gothic cathedral, the parliament buildings and the

8.00   FIND YOUR PARTNERS

8.30   FEED YOUR PARTNERS
onwards

9.30   TREASURE HUNT

10.00 DANCING

11.30 CAROLS

12.00 A STIRRUP-CUP

       AULD LANG SYNE

Bridge tables in the blue room upstairs for those who wish to play

Clifford Norton
&
Noël E. Norton

welcome you most warmly
& wish you a happy Christmas

Invitation to British Legation Christmas Party, 1943.

several high bridges which spanned the deep gorge of the river Aare were other features which made Berne such an interesting place. How lucky I felt to be there.

During this time I was able to reflect on my escape from Germany, via France, to Switzerland. I thanked my lucky stars that the autumn weather, which could be very cold in this region, had been kind to me. Luck plays quite a part in a successful escape and some of the incidents I have described amply bear this out. However, as success is often described as 10% luck and 90% hard work, I can say that during my walk I endeavoured to go steadily and carefully and tried to minimize the risk whenever possible. This I did by walking by night and hiding up by day. Walking at night is quite daunting at times and one comes across many situations where decisions have to be made on the spot and quick thinking and action are essential. On my walk I did not find myself living in constant fear. Of course, there were moments of apprehension, for example when seeking help. At such times I had to put some trust in the people from whom I was seeking assistance and likewise they had to put their trust in me. I will never forget their generous help as they had far more to lose than I had, if caught.

Gradually I recovered from my ordeal and after about a month Major Fryer asked me if I would like to have a job at the Legation. I was delighted to have the opportunity of doing something useful and so commenced full time work in the Foreign Office Section.

Living and working in Switzerland was very pleasant and the only restriction placed on me was that I had to report to the Swiss authorities once a month. The Air Ministry had been informed of my arrival in Switzerland and they in turn had notified my parents. As it had been eleven weeks since I was reported missing my family were obviously relieved to have official confirmation that I was safe, although they had already received the very welcome postcard from the Swiss soldier. As mail leaving Switzerland was examined by the Germans I was discouraged from writing home. With the permission of the Legation I did write a short letter soon after arriving in Berne and, on the few occasions when I did write home, I always let the authorities see my letter just to ensure that no information which could be of use to the enemy was unwittingly included.

Although Switzerland was a neutral country it was completely surrounded by enemy occupied territory and the Swiss had to obtain permission, from both the German and British authorities, to bring in supplies from other countries of the world. So while food was not as strictly rationed as in Britain there was rationing and one had to give up coupons for meals when eating in a restaurant.

Working at the Legation enabled me to make many new friends especially as there was such a good social life with many parties given by the Legation and by various members of the staff. One very good and interesting friend that I made was Harry Underwood who, in his spare-time, was the Swiss correspondent of *The Railway Gazette*. Of course, he was very knowledgeable on the Swiss railway system and during my stay in Switzerland we travelled extensively by train and I was able to see a great deal of the country. Harry Underwood was also a keen opera goer and I had the pleasure of attending many productions at the Berne Opera House as well as enjoying concerts at the Kursaal.

I kept in touch with Harry after the war and enjoyed many Swiss walking holidays with him. Thus I came to know the country, its history, customs and geography, very well.

Sport played an important part in my life in Berne. In winter ice-skating was popular and I used to join other members of the Legation staff on the ice rink early in the morning before going to work.

Later, two other R.A.F. escapers, Norman Watts and Norman Mackie joined me in Berne both of whom were keen golfers. One of my colleagues at the Legation was Mr. Harradine, whose peacetime job had been designing and building golf courses, and he introduced us to the Berne Golf Club where he was the professional. So we enjoyed many happy hours playing golf and receiving tuition on the delightful nine-hole course on top of the Gurten which was reached by funicular.

Another attraction was the Kegelbahn, or to the uninitiated, the nine-pin bowling alley. We regularly frequented a restaurant at the foot of the Gurten where there was a fine bowling alley. In the winter months we formed an R.A.F. team known as the 'Riff-Raffs' and consisting of Watts, Lamus, Lambert and myself. There were also two British Legation teams and two teams from the American Legation so league matches provided friendly competition. We had many happy evenings with beer and skittles.

Yet another sporting activity in which I participated was football and we managed to get together a team comprising my R.A.F. colleagues and the younger members of the various Legation Departments. Members of the Commercial Section had contacts with local businesses and we were able to arrange many fixtures with them.

With an interesting job and good friends, with parties, sport, opera and music and light entertainment at the Bier Keller my time in Switzerland was a very enjoyable experience and the time passed quickly.

British Legation Football Team, 1943.

I worked at the Legation for about fifteen months and could have remained in Switzerland until after the war but in due course I elected to try to get back to England when an opportunity arose.

Soon after I arrived in Switzerland, Vichy France had fallen to the Germans and this had made organized escapes from Switzerland more difficult and obviously it took some time before the escape routes were working again. In due course some of my R.A.F. friends left Switzerland on their way back to England and my turn came in January 1944.

The Last Lap

Great secrecy surrounded our departure from Berne. Neither I nor my seven travelling companions told anyone of our intended journey to England. We just 'disappeared' and, when we were safely across the Swiss border, Legation staff settled our hotel bills and collected up our personal belongings.

We left Berne by the evening train for Geneva. Once there we made our way to the frontier and, with the agreement of the Swiss authorities, crossed into France. We had been given instructions to walk a short distance to meet someone who would identify himself by a password. So, having done as we were told, we met our guide who took us to a waiting lorry. We all piled in and we set off for a small village a few miles from the border, outside the controlled zone. Here our party was divided up and four of us were taken to a small apartment in the village, the home of a lady and her young son, where we were to remain until the next stage of our journey. The other four members of our party were accommodated nearby at another safe house. The plan was to get out of France as quickly as possible by taking a train to a station about ten miles from the Spanish border and continuing on foot over the Pyrenees. Normally one would have expected the whole journey to have taken a couple of days.

However, things did not go according to plan and rumour had it that the Spanish end of the escape route had been broken. We just had to wait in our hide-out until such time as the line was said to be clear. It was an anxious period for us all being cooped up here, especially as we did not know exactly what had happened or, indeed, if the Germans knew of our presence. Much of our time was taken up playing cards and our only means of exercise was to leave the apartment after dark to walk in the countryside taking great care not to be seen. We managed quite well for food as we had brought money with us and our helper was able to buy provisions on the black market.

During the day we often saw German army vehicles passing the apartment and on one occasion, when the Maquis had blown up some trains in a marshalling yard near Annecy, there was great activity in the village.

As each week passed we enquired from our guide, who visited us periodically, when we were likely to move and every time we were told that it would probably be 'next week'. Although we appreciated the difficulties it was not surprising that we were becoming frustrated not knowing what was happening. Nearly a month passed and still we had no news. We were beginning to feel somewhat restless and nervous and we made up our minds that if we did not move fairly soon we would attempt to return to Switzerland and, as we were armed, would even shoot our way back if necessary. Anyhow we did not have to do this as, on his next visit, our guide told us that we would be moving in a day or so.

The son of our helper was a young lad of about 19 or 20

and he was very keen to go to England to join the Free French
Forces and so he decided to take his chance with us.

The next stage of our journey began when we were taken to
a nearby railway station where we were reunited with the rest
of our party. Our guide bought us tickets and we boarded a
night train that would take us near to the French/Spanish
border. We had been supplied with false identity papers and I
was supposed to be a commercial traveller by the name of
Jean Lambert.

For the first part of our journey we had to stand in a
crowded corridor along with German troops who were probably moving to a new camp or returning from leave. The
scene was reminiscent of wartime trains at home. When the
train stopped at Lyons one of these soldiers asked me a
question. Fortunately our guide was standing nearby and he
answered the soldier who was, I believe, merely enquiring in
which station the train was standing. It was a very uncomfortable moment. A little later we managed to find seats so we
settled down and pretended to sleep and drowsily showed our
tickets when the inspector came round, thus avoiding any
conversation. With some relief we finally reached Perpignan
but, as we walked up the platform towards the barrier, we saw
German officers standing there and we wondered whether
they were waiting for us. We walked past them as nonchantly
as possible but we felt that they were far too close for comfort. Perpignan was the nearest point to the Spanish frontier
to which one could travel by public transport without under-
going rigorous checks on one's papers.

We followed our guide from the station to a house nearby.
Here we were provided with a meal and met our Spanish
guide for the next stage of our journey. Our hostess, and
helper, was a schoolteacher who spoke English so we were

False Identity Card.

CERTIFICAT DE TRAVAIL　Mod. 1

délivré sous la responsabilité de :

Monsieur *Grands moulins du Rhône*
Qualité :

(l'Employeur indiquera son titre, la raison sociale et l'adresse de son Établissement)

1, Quai de la Gare d'Eau
Lyon

A *Lyon* le *1 octobre* 1943

Signature et cachet du Responsable :

GRANDS MOULINS DU RHONE
LYON

J. 37280-43. (8)　　　　　　　　T.S.V.P.

IDENTITÉ DU TITULAIRE

Nom et Prénoms *Lambert Jean*
Né le *4 février 1915* à *Lyon*

Adresse : *avenue Foch, 7.*
Lyon

Nationalité : *française*

exerçant { dans l'Établissement { ~~moins de 30 heures~~
{ ~~à son compte~~ { plus de 30 heures

(rayer les deux mentions inutiles)

le métier de *comptable*

depuis le *30 septembre 1943*

Inscrit dans la catégorie *2*
sous le N° *5*

J. Lambert

False Work Permit.

able to be well briefed on the next leg of our escape. We remained in the house until early evening and as darkness fell we set off on our trek across the Pyrenees to Spain. The crossing had to be made on foot because of the controls on the railway and roads at the frontier crossing points. Our first obstacle was encountered fairly soon after leaving Perpignan and this was the River Tech which we had to cross. As there was no bridge in the vicinity we had to undress and wade across while carrying our clothes above our heads. The water was about chest high and none too warm on a cold February night. As the river was not very wide we were soon across and after attempting to dry ourselves off as best we could, using our handkerchiefs, we quickly donned our clothes again and set off on the uphill journey over the Pyrenees.

Our guide was a small man, very fit and agile, and he reminded me of a mountain goat as he hurriedly scrambled up the hillside. This made the going difficult for many of us who only had ordinary shoes and not walking boots. The trouble was that the grassy surface on parts of the route made the soles of our shoes extremely slippery and so it was difficult to get a good grip and there was a lot of slipping and sliding. However, with the desire to get into Spain without delay our will-power kept us going. We only stopped occasionally for a rest on the uphill trek. Finally we reached the top which was a rather desolate area with many burnt trees which must have been the result of a forest fire. Some hundred yards on the guide indicated a point where the frontier was reputed to be but we only had his word for this. We went a little further and then sat down for a well earned rest and to our surprise our guide collected some wood and lit a small fire which was very comforting on this cold February night. Whilst he did not brew us a cup of tea he did let us have a squirt of red wine from his leather wine bottle. After our rest we put out the fire and made our way down to the foot of the Pyrenees, this time on the Spanish side.

As daylight broke our guide took us to his village which was no more than a collection of small igloo-like, mud huts. We entered one of these through a small opening and sat round a wood fire in the centre of the hut, the smoke escaping through a hole in the roof. It seemed as if these people were a type of gypsy or nomad who made baskets and similar articles from the reeds which grew around there.

We remained here all day and in the evening, as darkness fell, we were collected by another guide and taken to a nearby marshalling yard where the plan was to jump on a goods train as soon as it got under way. As I mentioned earlier, it was not possible to travel on passenger trains near the frontier because officials scrutinized travel documents. We spent a frustrating time waiting for the train to move off. We sat on a bank beside the track and our guide went off periodically to enquire when the train would leave. He would then return and tell us that it would be departing in a few minutes and then we would wait and wait. We went through this ritual a number of times before the great moment came. On continental goods trains there is a little guard's box at the end of each wagon and the object was to board the train as soon as it moved off and to install ourselves in one of these boxes.

Our party divided into pairs and my companion was Chief Petty Officer Tubby Lister. He had been in Colditz along with Chief Petty Officer Wally Hammond, who was also travelling with us, and they had escaped whilst being transferred to another prison. As the train moved off we clambered aboard and tried to get into the box. We found that the door was locked and so, as the train rumbled along, we climbed over

the buffers to the other side of the wagon to try the door on
that side. Again we found this locked and concluded that
someone must be inside. We thought that perhaps two of our
party had beaten us to this particular wagon, especially when
we saw a light as someone struck a match. We banged lustily
on the door, telling the occupants to open up but it took quite
a while before a very surprised man opened the door to see
what 'fools' were knocking on the door of a moving train. We
got inside and found that the man was a Spanish railway
worker going off duty. We tried to converse with him in our
broken French and discovered that he would be leaving the
train at the same place as us. Previously we had been told the
approximate time that our journey would take and the number
of stations through which we would pass. Once at our desti-
nation we were off the train quickly and taken by our guide to
a Spanish farmhouse where we remained for a couple of days.

Now that we were some distance from the frontier we could
travel on passenger trains with less chance of any checks and
our next objective was to reach the British Consulate in Barcelona by catching the early morning workers' train. Whilst
at the farmhouse we had to familiarize ourselves with the
route we would take from the station to the Consulate. It was
imperative to reach the Consulate without being spotted by
the Spanish police because the Spanish authorities were pro
German and they would not have hesitated in handing us back
to the Germans or putting us in a notorious Spanish prison
which would not be the most desirable place to end up.

In the early morning we left the farmhouse and went to the
local station, bought tickets and boarded the workers' train.
After a short journey we arrived in Barcelona and set off for
the Consulate as we had been instructed. We left the station
by a side exit and walked along a road for a short distance,

took a right fork and kept on the right hand side of the road until we saw the British Consulate. Our instructions were to get inside as soon as possible without being seen by any Spanish police who might be around. All went according to plan and once inside we considered ourselves safe as, technically, we were on British soil.

We were interrogated by the Consulate staff as a security precaution because it was not uncommon for Germans to try to infiltrate the system and reach England by this route. We were given temporary British passports and fixed up with accommodation at a small hotel in the town. Here we remained while permission was sought from the Spanish authorities for us to travel to Gibraltar.

While staying at this hotel we managed to see a little of Barcelona which seemed to be a hive of activity. We were amused by the overcrowded trams with as many people hanging on to the outside as there were people inside. On our first evening we returned to our hotel at what was to us quite a reasonable time, probably about 10 o'clock, only to find that the hotel was locked and we were unable to find a bell or anything with which to raise the night-porter. So we decided to telephone the hotel and off we went to the local post office where there were 'phones. We could not make the telephone work with our Spanish money and after some enquiries discovered that one had to use tokens which, fortunately, we managed to obtain. We finally made our call to the hotel and arranged for the door to be opened for us.

After a few days, arrangements having been made with the Spanish authorities, we left Barcelona by an early morning train for Madrid. It was a very pleasant journey and we were able to see much of the Spanish countryside which was surprisingly barren in places. It was also a considerable relief to be travelling legally with all one's papers in order. In Madrid we had a few hours to wait for our train to Gibraltar and so we were taken to the British Embassy and, as usual, we were interrogated.

We caught the night train to Algeciras and the next morning we reached the Spanish frontier and entered Gibraltar where we were questioned yet again. We spent a week awaiting transport to England. There were not many planes to the United Kingdom and so the more important people had priority and we just had to wait until seats were available. Our few days in Gibraltar were quite relaxing and we saw what there was to be seen of this outpost of the British Empire.

Eventually my turn came to travel home and I boarded a Dakota for a night flight. The route had to be out over the Atlantic, outside Spanish air space, and it was not a very comfortable flight. It was extremely bumpy and at one point the plane hit a turbulent air pocket and threw many of us out of our seats. The first thought that crossed my mind was, what an end to an escape to find oneself in the middle of the Atlantic Ocean. However, my worst fears were not borne out and we managed to sort ourselves out and get comfortable again for the remainder of the journey although it was so cold that blankets were handed out to keep the passengers warm.

Early next morning, the 24th February 1944, we arrived in Bristol and again I was interrogated just to ensure that I was a bona fide R.A.F. escaper. I was back in England 18 months after setting off from Suffolk to bomb Nuremburg. After leaving Bristol my next stop was London where I had a final interrogation at the Marylebone Headquarters of M19. This was a much more detailed enquiry just to make absolutely sure that I was the person I claimed to be. Then for the Air

Ministry I had to go over the complete story of events from
the time I took off from Stradishall for the raid on Nuremburg
until I arrived in Switzerland.

Latter Days

Following my final debriefing I was given leave and told to await instructions. After about two weeks I had to report to Morecambe where I rejoined the R.A.F. and was kitted out. I then awaited my next posting which was to Air Warfare Analysis Section located near Stanmore in Middlesex. It was primarily a Civil Service unit which was involved with the preparation of maps, for use with radar, and intelligence work including the photographing of possible enemy targets such as rocket sites, gun sites, marshalling yards, etc. One aspect of the work with which I, and a number of other R.A.F. personnel, had to be acquainted was blind bombing techniques using radar, so that we could join an operational group, in my case No. 2 Group Tactical Air Force, to do any necessary calculations for their squadrons. Soon after the D-Day landings four of us joined No. 2 Group Headquarters at Wallingford and later went to Brussels when the German armies had retreated. Our aircraft operated from Melsbroek airfield and the Headquarters staff were housed at a large Belgium military barracks in Brussels. Just before the Germans capitulated we were moved up to Osnabruck in case the aircraft were needed to attack targets in northern Germany.

From: Air Vice Marshal Sir Thomas ELMHIRST,
K.B.E., C.B., A.F.C.,

Tel. No. ABBEY 3411.
Ext. 5792/3.

AIR MINISTRY,
KING CHARLES STREET.
WHITEHALL, S.W.1.

ACAS(I)/238A/46.

8 August, 1946.

Dear Colhoun,

      To develop in the Royal Air Force the tradition that aircrew never accept capture, it is proposed to form a panel of famous escapers and evaders to lecture two or three times a year.

      Your escape is an excellent example of the indomitable spirit which we are endeavouring to pass on to present day aircrew.

      Would you please let me know whether you are able to join this panel of lecturers?

      It is hoped that Air Ministry will be able to defray the expenses involved if you are able to lecture.

Yours sincerely,

T.W. Elmhirst

Letter from Air Vice Marshall Sir Thomas Elmhirst, 1946.

However, this was but a short stay as after a week or two the war in Europe was over and we returned to our Headquarters in Belgium once more.

During the latter part of the war, when I was stationed in Brussels, I had to travel to London occasionally to collect maps and on one of my trips I met an R.A.F. officer who had interrogated me at the Air Ministry on my return from Switzerland. He recognized me as I passed through Croydon airport and asked me what decoration I had been awarded for my escape and was somewhat surprised when I told him that I had receiving nothing. In fact, the only slight recognition that I received was a letter from Air Vice Marshal Sir Thomas Elmhirst, in August 1946, telling me that 'your escape is an excellent example of the indomitable spirit which we are endeavouring to pass on to present day aircrew' and inviting me 'to join a panel of famous escapers and evaders to lecture two or three times a year'.

As soon as the war in Europe was over I sought permission from my Commanding Officer, Air Vice Marshal Sir Basil Embry, himself a noted escaper, to go to Boulay in an attempt to find my first helpers. Permission was granted and I set off for France with two companions. We soon found the farm at Rinange, the home of Armand and Marie Esch and their daughters, Olga, Odile and Emmy. It was a wonderful reunion and a lot of time was spent reminiscing about the time Jim Dixon and I had spent with them when they were under German occupation.

More than fifty years later I am still in touch with the Esch family. M. Esch died in 1963 but I was able to visit Mme. Esch until her death in 1985. Various members of their family have visited England and I have met all M. and Mme. Esch's grandchildren and many of their great grandchildren.

M. and Mme. Esch and their three daughters at Rinange, 1945.

Unfortunately, I was never able to visit my other helpers as I did not know their names or exactly where they lived.

As for the rest of my crew, they were all taken prisoner. Jim Dixon was very badly treated by German workers at the farm where we were separated and eventually ended up in a prisoner of war camp in Silesia with fellow crew members Jock Skinner, Jimmy Mullineaux and Alan Cook. At this camp members of the R.A.F. were picked out for particularly harsh treatment and at one stage they were chained up for twelve hours a day. Had I been captured at the same time as Jim Dixon I have no doubt that I would have suffered the same fate. Jimmy Mullineaux and Alan Cook made several unsuccessful attempts to escape and finally Alan Cook was shot in 1943 whilst trying to get away from a working party. He is buried in Cracow Cemetary in Poland. Jim Dixon died in 1990 never having fully recovered from the hardship he endured as a prisoner of war.

Our pilot, Peter Harper, was held in a different camp and I trust he survived the war for it was his skill in landing our Wellington which ensured our survival.

I have read many escape stories and talked to many escapers but there are few who have crossed occupied France without help from the Resistance and even fewer who have walked out of Germany without having first been in a prisoner of war camp.